TOXIC RELATION

Developed 1997 from the KEYS TO FREEDOM EDUCATIONAL WORKSHOP SERIES

Library of Congress Cataloging-in-Publication of Data TXu1-808-621

Key Insights Publishing through ASCAP Registry #6657260

Scripture References and quotations from King James Version of the Bible unless otherwise indicated

Cover Design: Worship Media Group [Mywmg.com]

For speaking engagements or training sessions, contact:

Kingdom Keys Apostolic Hub or Key Insights, LLC
(313) 610-4626
keyinsightstraining@gmail.com

DEDICATION

This book is a culmination of the wisdom gained through many life lessons. I would need way too many pages to include all of the people who attributed to such. However, my sons Donald, Aaron, and Steven and my daughter Karrie as well as married life, have contributed a great deal to my mental and spiritual growth. I want to thank my husband, Michael Morgan for his love, support, and patience.

I am quite thankful for my parents, Frances Carson (Jeannie) and my father Donald Watson (Duck) who have gone on to be with the Lord; they brought me into the world in the precious years of their youth, and for my grandmother (Nanny) who raised me.

My prayer is that all teens, and all of my grandchildren and great grandchildren get a chance to read this book prior to dating.

TABLE OF CONTENTS

About the Author

Pamela Jean Morgan is a native Detroiter and is married to Michael Kevin Morgan. She is the mother of 4 adult children from a previous marriage. She began seeking and searching for something to validate her at the young age of 13 years old; she went looking for love in all the wrong places. Finally, at the age of 21 years old, she thought she had found the answer to her deep inner thirst, which was marriage. When there was no peace found in the marriage, she went to church to get God to "fix it". After saying the salvation prayer and going through the motions of becoming a Christian, the marriage still was not magically fixed. Well, six years later, after saying the salvation prayer and receiving the gift of speaking in other tongues; Pam began to use cocaine and eventually became a crack cocaine addict, although she had confessed Christ as her Savior. Several years later she had come to the end of the 'drug-using' road, only to find that drugs were not her only problem, and the deep inner thirst was still there.

She found that she indeed had *Another Addiction – Toxic Relationships*. No matter how many times she "fell in love" she was still empty. It was upon this realization that God posed a question to her; ***"Is It Love or Are You Just Thirsty?*** and the journey began. She began her pursuit for wholeness, holiness and happiness: not through men, not through drugs, not even through Church; this time she pursued wholeness through a relationship with Christ.

Through her relationship with Christ, she has found the true and living water to finally satisfy that deep inner thirst. She has also found her purpose in the Body of Christ both within the local assembly as well as in the community. Her achievements, since God rescued her from the horrors of addictions, include earning a Master Degree in Business Administration, Bachelors in Human Services and various certifications from the Michigan Board of Addiction

Professionals. As owner of Key Insights LLC, Morgan is a nationally known professional development trainer and substance abuse professional - providing services since 1993.

Pamela Morgan, has accepted her call from God. She is an ordained minister of the Gospel of Jesus Christ, operating in her calling to serve the Body of Christ in whatever capacity pleases the Lord. She is a two-time pancreatic cancer survivor and experiences miracle after miracle as God triumphantly walks her through life challenges. God sent His word to heal her and to deliver her out of her destruction. He set her apart from a profane life and ordained her to use His Word to root out strongholds, pull down imaginations, tear-down the walls holding His people in bondage and to plant His Truth in their hearts, that they may be built into a fruitful vine, equipping God's people with the keys to gain freedom from various bondages, empowering them with insight to emerge into their destiny.

A FEW POINTS TO PONDER:

1. Many readers will undergo deliverance.
2. You will need a notebook to journal your thoughts, hurts, discoveries, and revelations.
3. You will need an accountability partner to assist you in this deliverance process.
4. My suggestion is that your accountability partner be someone who has a working relationship with God, strives to live by spiritual principles, has been set free from toxic relationship involvement, and strives to live a lifestyle of making Spirit led choices such as choosing God's will over self-willed/self-gratifying choices.
5. The accountability partner needs to be a non-judgmental person with whom you have no romantic attraction.

6. Spending small amounts of time socializing with your accountability partner is suggested so that you do not replace the old relationship with the new relationship with your accountability partner.
7. During this process of deliverance, you will let go of old lifestyles, old relationships and habits; there will emerge a need to replace them and the replacement must be God, not another person, place or thing.
8. Moving forward, the confusion concerning your experiences in relationships will begin to dissipate.
9. You will need to take notes as the Holy Spirit reveals Truth to you. You will see repetition in your behavior as well as unhealthy beliefs and traditions, which have led to poor choices.
10. God is going to expedite time, catapulting you into His purpose for your life as you turn to Him.

[According to 2 Corinthians 3:16 (*NIV*), whenever anyone turns to the Lord; the veil is taken away.]

11. He is untying you to ride into the lives of many, just as he untied the donkey to ride into Jerusalem. The Master has need of you and He will use everything that you have done and everything that was done to you for your good and His Glory as you fall deeper in love with Him; ALL things work together for the good of those who love God who are called according to His purpose.

Expect to see His Kingdom come on earth as it is in Heaven, in your life.

We cannot do this alone; Let's go to the throne of grace where we may obtain mercy and find grace to help in this time of need:

<u>Prayer</u>: Lord remove the veil from my eyes as I turn my heart to you in the areas I have been holding on to. Lord, I am thoroughly beaten by my old ways and habits. I am willing to do whatever it takes to be free. I desire to journey with you to see what you see and hear what you hear

concerning me and the future You have for me. Father, I know You love me. Help me to fall deeper in love with You. Father God, open up the eyes of my understanding that I may know who You say that I am. Help me to know and appreciate who I am to You and who You are to me. Give me eyes to see what You see concerning me and ears to hear Your thoughts towards me; thoughts of good and not of evil. Father, help me to know what your plan for my life is. Help me to find my worth in who I am to You. I want to be made whole. Give me courage to face and forgive my past and the ability to accept where I am today so that I can move into the future You have predestined for me. Father, I want You to be glorified in my life. Amen

PREFACE

Every human being has an inner thirst. We all begin our quest for wholeness at different points in our lives; but generally, near the age of puberty. We were created with a void in our spirit which was designed to cause us to seek wholeness and satisfaction through a relationship with God. This wholeness and holiness provided by God relieves us of our obsession to use other things or other people to give us that false sense of wholeness and gratification. However, along the way of life, most of us seek satisfaction and wholeness through avenues other than relationship with God, not realizing that the only way to truly be whole is through relationship with God and with self. For many of us, relationships have been the avenue through which we pursued happiness – only to end up in one toxic relationship after another. So, I ask you, Is It Love or Are You Just Thirsty?

Entering relationships without first being made whole is a recipe for toxic relationships. We seek love only to find that we are attempting to satisfy an insatiable deep inner thirst designed to be watered only by God's living water. Nevertheless, we continue in our fruitless pursuit of happiness through relationships, only to become addicted to the other person or at the very least; addicted to the idea of being happy. In time, we may look back only to find a trail of promiscuity or perhaps history of a longstanding abusive relationship of which we have refused to let go of. How paradoxical; we become more fragmented as we seek wholeness and relief from our fragmented state of being.

Addiction is threefold: physical, mental and spiritual. The physical and mental aspects will continually engulf the addicted person if the spiritual aspect is not addressed first. There are however some physical changes that must be put into place in order to improve our mental state. With practical solutions, clear directives, life experiences and answers to some commonly asked questions; this book will assist in ending the vicious relationship addiction cycle and will find satisfaction for that inner thirst.

A POEM TO PONDER

(a bit of my testimony)

"I'M BLESSED"

I'm a little girl, I've always got a curl - Grandma fixes me up real pretty,

But sometimes I am so-so sad, Oh what a pity

Mama's gone, only God knows where, sometimes it seems she doesn't care

Oh! When will she return? And Dad, to him I don't exist

He doesn't come around, not even for a kiss.

I'd really like a dad like others have, oh! Now I'm fast approaching twelve.

But I'm still a little girl, I've always got a curl and Grandma fixes me up real pretty

But sometimes I am so, so sad, oh! what a pity, if only I had a Dad.

Now I'm 28, this life is all in vain. I feel really empty with lots of pain.

I've gotta do something to ease this pain, I'll begin to use cocaine.

There's a void in me, an empty space; I thank God for His saving Grace

Well, life goes on, I cannot die, not even with my greatest try.

I used to live and live to use – I try to fill that space.

I use drugs, money and men but I'm still losing the race.

Now I'm 36 and I've met a man and this is what He said:

"OH, CHILD OF MINE, WHEN WILL YOU SEE; YOU'RE CHOSEN, YOU BELONG TO ME

THOUGH YOU WERE LONELY AND OH SO SAD, I WAS THERE TO BE YOUR DAD.

I KEPT YOU CLOSE UNDER MY WING, I PROTECTED YOU FROM MANY A THING.

YES, TRULY YOU WENT THROUGH SOME TOUGH TIMES AND I AM SURE YOU HAVE YOUR 'WHYS'

NEVER MIND ALL THE 'WHYS', I WAS THERE TO DRY YOUR EYES

OH CHILD, OH CHILD WHEN WILL YOU SEE, YOU BELONG TO ME"

He filled the void and took the pain, there's no more need, to use cocaine,

He teaches me how to be content in whatever state I'm in,

Life's no longer all in vain, He teaches me how to win. When I am heavy burdened, He gives me rest

Oh, I tell you, He's the best. He'll never leave me nor forsake me, I love Him for He first loved me.

OH CHILD, OH CHILD YOU FINALLY SEE – THAT YOU BELONG TO ME!

Psalms 10:14 "The helpless put their trust in God. He is the helper of the fatherless."

CHAPTER I:

INTRODUCTION: WHAT IS A TOXIC RELATIONSHIP AND HOW IS IT ANOTHER ADDICTION

"…for a man is a slave to whatever controls him." II Peter 2:19

A toxic relationship is a relationship that ultimately makes you sick emotionally, physically and/or spiritually. Toxic relationships generally precede, follow or co-exist with substance abuse and/or some other form of self-destruction, suicide included. Relationships can be a terribly painful area because we tend to place unrealistic expectations on ourselves and others. (Narcotic Anonymous Basic text) The pain of relationships is often so great that there is a need to relieve the pain unnaturally such as with drugs, alcohol (which is a drug) or another relationship. People who are addicted to toxic relationships find themselves doing things that they never would have imagined they would do. They find themselves putting up with ridiculous behavior or behaving ridiculously themselves, in a desperate effort to maintain the relationship. For many, the relationship leads to the use of mood-altering chemicals such as alcohol, narcotics, barbiturates, tranquilizers, antidepressants, etc.; these are used to avoid coming to terms with the reality of the relationship.

Relationship addicts become addicted to relationships more so than to the actual person. Although the person may seem to be indispensable, if he or she leaves the relationship, they will be replaced with someone who soon becomes just as significant because the goal is to "never be alone". The three (3) major aspects of addiction are physical compulsion, mental obsession and spiritual self-centeredness caused by the inner void. When a person has become addicted to the relationship, they experience an extreme sense of emptiness, incompleteness and despair and a sense of abandonment when the other person is either not available or not acting in the manner they desire. The mental aspect of the addiction becomes apparent when the person becomes obsessed with the need to fill the void and believes that everything will be alright as long as they can connect and remain connected to their significant other. At the point of believing this to be true, they are now willing to do themselves a great deal of damage to obtain and maintain the condition of being connected. This obsessive behavior becomes compulsive in that once they start seeking the connection to the other person, they cannot experience any lasting satisfaction and the quest becomes insatiable and unending. The spiritual aspect is characterized by the self-centered efforts driven by the overwhelming need to fill the inner void, even when it means hurting, violating, endangering or disrespecting self and/or others. Relationship addicts cannot develop good relationships and even when situations arise that require to live without a significant other, they quickly get into another relationship.

STAGES OF ADDICTIVE DISEASE AS APPLICABLE TO RELATIONSHIPS

Clinically speaking we can see toxic relationship addiction as it is related to addictive disease in 1956 the American Medical Association formally identified addiction as a disease. [American Medical Association, 1956] Addictive diseases manifest themselves in many areas such as gambling, shopping, food, drugs (including alcohol) and relationships. As we explore toxic relationships as another addiction, you will see similarities to substance abuse and other addictions. Because of this, when a person has an addiction, they must deal with the addictive disease rather than just discontinuing indulgence in the identified addiction. If they stop with just simply abstaining and not dealing with the disease, they will transfer addictions, thereby giving place to it in another area. Addiction professional Howard Shafer developed the six stages of addiction change. [*Howard J. Shaffer, PhD, CAS*]

We will look at those stages as they relate to relationships. Stage One is the Emergence of the Addiction. This is the initial onset where a person begins to indulge, and experience good feelings. For a person addicted to relationships, this could begin as early as puberty. A time when an adolescent is feeling awkward, perhaps rejected, and may be experiencing problems within the family unit. When he or she begins to get attention from someone who expresses interest in them, good feelings cause them to pursue attention which may result in sexual activity. Although the adolescent was not necessarily seeking sex, the attention seemed to make it all worth it. What has happened is that the inner void, the place designed for God to dwell, has been tapped into by a human. This person begins to experience a false sense of acceptance and worth.

Then they enter Stage Two, which is Positive Consequences. As strange as it may seem rape, molestation and incest have often led to ongoing consented indulgence;

because the individual is so spiritually and emotionally thirsty, they feed off of the temporary euphoria, settling for brief moments of a false sense of contentment and security. Whether it is an adolescent or an adult relationship, the stages of addiction are the same. The positive consequences stage may include social acceptance, emotional euphoria (which is a feeling of intoxication) and a false sense of self-esteem. Inevitably, the person must advance to the third stage because sin is only pleasurable for a season.

Stage Three is Adverse Consequences; this begins when painful and uncomfortable consequences emerge. Initially this is a difficult stage to accept because there are positive consequences occurring simultaneously. The addicted person may deny that the adverse consequences are directly related to their involvement in the relationship. The friends of the addicted person may see the adverse effects much clearer because they are unbiased in their perspective. In other words, they are standing far enough off from the relationship that they can see the bigger picture.

Stage Four is the evolution of quitting, the turning point. This is where adverse consequences enter the individual's awareness and they become very indecisive, breaking it off perhaps several times only to give in to their desires and/or the desires of the other person by re-entering the relationship. They may continue this cycle until the adverse consequences become overwhelming. This is the point in which the individual hits bottom and declares that enough is enough. Then emerges Stage Five which is the Quitting Stage. This stage puts a great deal of emphasis on actions such as avoiding contact with the person, seeking outside help and reorganizing their lifestyle to exclude activities which formally accompanied the relationship. Stage Six is the Relapse Prevention or Change Maintenance Stage. This stage involves the use of new skills and new lifestyle patterns, enabling the individual to remain free from toxic relationships.

Spiritually speaking, 'we are slaves to whatever controls us' according to II Peter 2:19. Romans 6:16 (AMP), 'if you continually surrender yourselves to anyone to do his will, you are the slaves of him whom you obey whether that be to sin which leads to death or to obedience which leads to righteousness which is right standing with God.' God told us through the Prophet Jeremiah that 'our own wickedness will correct us, and our backsliding shall reprove us' (Jer. 2:19). We see that God has predestined man to become bound by whatever he chooses over Him. Whatever we choose to obey apart from God's will for us ultimately becomes our master, taking us into captivity and thereby teaching us that we should obey God. In other words, the very thing we disobey God with to get what we want will correct us; causing us so much pain, we will be forced to let go and run back to God. At some point in our backsliding, we learn to appreciate, respect, and accept God's will and direction even if we would rather have something else. Whether we refer to this as addictive disease or simply sin, we see it as progressive and only pleasurable for a season; eventually bringing forth death. It becomes our master and we become its slave. Our own transgressions will correct us, teaching us to let the relationship go.

SELF ASSESSMENT – IS MY RELATIONSHIP TOXIC?

QUIZ YOURSELF: here is a 20-point true or false questionnaire. Honesty is the key here. Be true to your own self. Your willingness to be honest will determine your ability to get free. Honesty is the first key to freedom from the chains of toxic relationships: another addiction. Perhaps you'll want to record your answers in your journal as a beginning mark of your journey towards wholeness.

Answer True or False:

1. In relationships, I ignore problems and pretend they aren't happening.

2. I pretend things are not really bad, trying to believe a change will come tomorrow.

3. I do not feel content & peaceful with myself, In fact, I feel empty & void.

4. I latch onto people and/or things that I think can provide me with happiness.

5. The thought of losing whoever becomes my source of happiness, I feel terribly threatened.

6. When that source is not available, oftentimes I feel a gut twisting, hand wringing anxious feeling in the pit of my stomach.

7. It is hard for me to believe others really love me.

8. I desperately seek love and approval, oftentimes from people who are incapable of loving anyone,

including themselves.

9. I latch onto people just because they say they want or need me, instead of taking the time to see if they are good for me.

10. Someone loving or liking me is enough to constitute grounds for a relationship, even if I do not particularly like them, I like the attention.

11. For the most part, I look to relationships to provide me with my good feelings.

12. I lose interest in my own life when I “fall in love”.

13. I have a fear of being rejected or left alone so I tolerate abuse to keep people from leaving me.

14. When my significant other is not ‘acting right’, I feel a sense of emptiness, incompleteness and despair.

15. I find myself putting up with ridiculous behavior or behaving ridiculously to maintain my relationship.

16. When I find someone else interested in me, I am

able to leave the abusive relationship for the next relationship.

17. My view of myself is contingent on how others view me.

18. When no one else is interested in me, I feel unwanted and worthless.

19. The excitement (the euphoric high) always wears off, then the empty feeling returns.

20. Whenever I am in a relationship, I cannot think or talk about anything else; even when I appear to be conversing with someone else, my mind is on the object of my obsession.

How did you do? If you answered 'true' to at least half of the statements above, you have the right book. When the Lord began to deal with me concerning toxic relationships, I answered true to all of these statements. I suffered from a grave degree of sickness in the area of relationships. When I stopped smoking crack cocaine little did I know that the journey had just begun. I thank God for not leaving me blinded by my emotions and hindered by my past.

My relationship addiction greatly resembled the crack cocaine addiction of which God had set me free from. To get free from toxic relationships, I followed the same pattern I had followed to obtain and maintain my freedom from crack. I experienced all of the stages of addiction and finally "hit bottom." I became ready to have God help me with relationship problems. The first thing I had to do was get honest with God and another human being. I had to do what the word of God says in James 5:16; '*confess your faults one to another and pray for one another that you may be healed.*' I had to admit that my ways had failed me miserably. I had to become specific about the sins I had committed and the bondage I was still in. "God, I have sinned," is too vague. Now is your time to speak out loud to God. Here are some statements which may express how you feel. If they apply to you, confess them. If not, add your own.

i. I feel like I'm nothing without a mate.

ii. I base who I am on who wants me.

iii. I feel bad about doing ________________ in my desperate attempt to keep from being rejected and left alone. [Fill in the blank]

iv. I'm afraid of being alone.

v. I've committed fornication (sex outside of marriage).

vi. I've committed adultery (sex with a person married to someone else, or someone other than my spouse).

vii. I'm ruled by my sexual desires.

viii. I'm addicted to pornography.

ix. I stay in an abusive relationship for financial benefit and I know God has told me to leave.

x. I'm being abused but I'm afraid to let go.

xi. Other (add your own) ___________________ [Fill in the blank].

POINTS TO PONDER:

1. Ask God to forgive you.
2. Confess to your accountability partner and ask them to pray for you that you may be healed. I know it sounds like a lot but when you are sick and tired of being in bondage; in your self-made prison, you become willing to obey the Word of God, no matter what extremes seem necessary to get free. Oftentimes we are afraid to talk openly with God (who already knows) and especially fearful of telling another person. God has not given you the 'spirit' of fear but power, love and a sound mind, so be courageous. Courage is not the absence of fear; courage is pushing past the fear. PUSH!!!!!!
3. Do not rationalize by saying, "God already knows so why must I say it?" Well, is power in confession; there is power in obeying the

scriptures and God says, "*Confess*" (*James 5:16*)

4. God is not angry because we have made unhealthy choices. He knows our condition is such that we cannot do good consistently without depending on Him.
5. He knows honesty is the key to moving forward into the destiny he has planned for us. In the book of Jeremiah 2:35 (*TLB*), God says to Israel, "*How you plot and scheme to win your lovers. The most experienced harlot could learn a lot from you...And yet you say, I haven't done anything wrong, surely God isn't angry with me! God's reply: You will receive consequences because you SAY you have not sinned.*" He gets angry when we don't get honest.
6. God is not surprised by any of our choices. He knew you before you were formed in your

mother's womb and yet He called you out of eternity into time, for His purpose, for His Glory. God is going to get great Glory from your life.

7. He knows our actions have been dictated by our pain. We have got to be honest about our pain. God has taken vengeance on all of the oppressors of our lives; the enemy's tactics used to dictate our poor choices in relationships. Our oppressors include rejection, abandonment, abuse, pride, fear, etc; we will address these and more as we move further into the journey. Again, God only gets angry if we won't be honest.
8. Stop blaming and justifying our choices based on our experiences that left wounds and scars.
9. Looking for love in all the wrong places; looking for love! Love was something I could

not identify. How can you find an egg at an easter egg hunt if you do not know what an egg is?

10. The exact nature of your wrong-doings. Now is the time to admit to the exact nature of your wrong-doings. How many times have you left a toxic relationship only to return under the illusion that it will be different this time or maybe you did not go back, but got into another one just as toxic. Guess what?
11. Your Chooser is broke. If you keep doing what you have always done, you will keep getting what you have always gotten.
12. Honesty exposes lies to the light of Truth where they must die.
13. Honesty stunts the growth of ungodly habits and attitudes.
14. Honesty is the antidote to this vicious cycle.

15. It is kind of like being lost in the shopping mall, in order to get the help that you need, you must first admit that you are lost. Then if you find a map in the center of the mall, you must identify your whereabouts by finding the button that says, "you are here." You now know where you are in relation to where you are trying to go.
16. Perhaps the ultimate goal in all relationships has been to be satisfied and feel 'right'.
17. Perhaps you have been "in love" on more occasions than you care to admit.
18. Was it love or were you just thirsty?
19. Once you admit that you are lost, you can begin mapping your course according to God given directions and you are well on your way.
20. Now I ask you, where are you? **IS IT LOVE OR ARE YOU JUST THIRSTY?**

NOTES AND PRAYERS

CHAPTER II:

IS IT LOVE OR ARE YOU JUST THIRSTY?

...To those who are in spiritual darkness – Come forth, show yourselves [come into the light of the Sun of Righteousness] ...They will not hunger or thirst, neither will mirage [mislead] or scorching wind or sun smite them, for He Who has mercy on them will lead them and by springs of water will He guide them (Isaiah 49:9 AMP)

The Body of Christ is in the stage of birthing, a time of purpose. Satan will keep us from advancing and destroying his kingdom as long as he can keep us seeking avenues apart from God to address our dehydration.

MISLED BY MIRAGES AND HALLUCINATIONS?

The scripture above is a promise of God's restoration. It indicates that when we are in darkness, we are hungry and thirsty; thereby may be misled by mirages. For this reason, I ask – *IS IT LOVE OR ARE YOU JUST THIRSTY?* Wow, what a question! We live in a 'quick fix' society. Let's face it, we may even microwave an egg from time to time. More often than not, we are trapped by our need for instant gratification. We want to feel good fast! In pursuing a relationship with God, the degree of desired satisfaction comes slowly, the process may be uncomfortable (due to the personal inner work involved) and progress is somewhat unrecognizable in the beginning. There is no instant gratification therefore we may grow impatient. The inner thirst may drive us to seek a relationship with a human being to get gratified instantly.

Let us look at the definition of thirst: an eager, famishing, all-consuming craving; a strong desire or discomfort caused by a need. What produces thirst? Thirst is produced by an unmet need. Looking for love in all the wrong places is a commonly heard phrase. Oftentimes, the one looking does not know what love looks like, however, humans instinctively want to be loved. They may think they have found 'love', only to find that it is not 'love' at all. Because of an emotional and spiritual void in their lives, they have in fact become dehydrated; thirsting after anything or anybody to 'make them feel better'.

Ezekiel 16:28, 33-34 (*TLB*) speaks to the issue of emptiness as it reads, *"...you have prostituted yourselves...it seems you can never find enough new lovers...Prostitutes charge for their services but not you. You give gifts to your lovers, bribing them to come to you...so you are the opposite of other prostitutes. No one pays you; instead, you pay them.*

We persist in our self-willed ways, seeking fulfillment apart from God. Ultimately, we give of ourselves, our possessions, and our peace in our desperate attempt to find satisfaction; only to be left wanting in the end. The behavior referenced in Ezekiel 16 caused this response from God – *'How you plot and scheme to win your lovers...the most experienced harlot could learn a lot from you' (Jeremiah 2:33)* He continues in verse 36... *'First here, then there you flit from one ally to another, asking for help – But your new friends in Egypt will let you down, just as Assyria did before. In despair, you will be led into exile with your hands on your head; for the Lord has rejected the ones you trust. You will not succeed despite their aid.'*

As it was for them, so it is for us. God will not allow our wrong ways to work for us, He has made it plain, *'You shall have no other gods before Me.'* The eager famishing all-consuming craving and strong desire has caused obscured vision. A person in a desert for a long period of time without water, becomes very thirsty; even dehydrated. As they are experiencing dehydration (depleted of water, drained, sucked dry) even a simple drink of water just will not suffice. A glass of water will not address their need. Their tongue feels very dry and they think they simply need a drink of water to address this external symptom. The truth is, they need an IV with proper nutrients to address an internal condition. When a woman is in childbearing labor, she becomes very thirsty. The dryness of her mouth tells her she needs water; however, the nurse gives her ice chips to pacify her while administering the needed nutrients through an IV. Extreme dehydration produces mirages and hallucinations. A mirage is an optical illusion in which distant objects appear to be nearby. A hallucination is the apparent perception of sights and sounds that are not actually present. Here is a moment of truth, what have you been pacifying yourself with? To pacify is to appease, to reduce to a submissive or tranquil state *(Merriam Webster)*.

Do this exercise by filling in the blank:

I have been pacifying myself with

____

Answer this question:

Haven't I been settling for ice chips long enough?

____

That person in the desert sees mirages and hallucinations of pools of water and rescuers when in fact, there really is nothing there but grains of sand. They may run up to the mirage of water, bend down and begin to put it to their mouths, only to find it cannot satisfy their thirst because it is indeed only sand. The same holds true for the person in need of love. They have been without love perhaps their entire lives. Perhaps they have never developed a relationship with God, although they may have been in church for most of their lives. Sometimes we confuse fellowshipping with people with a relationship with God. Humans have what can be called a God shaped void. This void, when not addressed with a relationship with God, produces a deep inner thirst that I see as an inward spiritual condition that manifests itself as a physical need, thereby the thirsty person begins to see what they feel they need to address the need. When they see potential significant others, they see what they need that person to be instead of seeing who and what that person truly is. This spiritual condition causes this thirst, this dehydrated state to be camouflaged as love, just as the sand appeared to be water. Think of times when you started out believing this was the absolute perfect person for you. The one you have been waiting for all of your life. Then months, maybe years later, you wonder what was wrong with you. Whatever possessed you to get involved with this person? Was it love or were you just thirsty?

Think about it. See if you can identify with the following assessment:

1. In the beginning stages, being with my significant other made me feel better.
2. I did not feel lonely anymore.
3. I felt confident and more intelligent.
4. I began to see myself as sexy and appealing.
5. I felt powerful. As the relationship progressed, I kept seeking the good feelings, but I experienced loneliness again.
6. I felt like a loser instead of confident.
7. I began regretting my actions and I hated what I was doing, but I could not stop.

8. I became angry with myself for continuing something that was obviously hurting me and depression would set it.
9. I became fearful of being totally alone again and I found myself becoming obsessive and controlling.
10. The more I try to control the relationship, the more depression I experience.
11. I really could not see my way out. I felt hopeless.

This is a portion of a self-assessment; this portion is used to assist substance abusers in identifying their addiction to drugs. How did you do? Are you beginning to see toxic relationships as another addiction? Insanity is doing the same thing over and over, expecting different results. How long must you eat dirt before you figure out that your emotions are playing tricks on you. Perhaps you should address that deep inner thirst with the only solution that can fulfill your need.

ONLY WATER TRULY SATISFIES THIRST.

Only water truly satisfies thirst; you can drink kool-aid, pop, alcohol, and wine and remain thirsty until you get a drink of water. Throughout scripture, we see references to the use of water by God in various forms, as the Holy Spirit and as the Word. We are to be sanctified and cleansed with the washing of water by the Word (*Ephesians 5:25*) and rivers of living waters shall flow out of our bellies if we go to Jesus when we thirst (*John 7:37*).

Why such reference to water? Well, let's look at the natural use of water. It is the most important thing in our lives next to air. Blood is approximately 90% water, over 2/3 of the human body is water, and our muscles contain 80-90% water. Loss of 20% may result in death. Water carries waste materials away from living cells, cleansing from filth. It is with the living Word of God. As a temperature regulator, water cools the body down in the form of perspiration, carrying inner heat out of the body. If we submit to the Holy Spirit in times of conflict, anger and other extreme emotions, He will prevent overheating, carry inner heat out of our spirit, bring the Word of Truth to our remembrance, and give us the ability to obey the Word and resist the devil; thus, cooling us down. Water distributes the food needed to live throughout the body. It is the Holy Spirit; He gives life. We need the Holy Spirit to distribute the food of the Word to those areas where we hunger and thirst. The Holy Spirit carries the Word to areas of bondage and desolation; bringing healing and deliverance. Here is an example: When we read about forgiveness, the Holy Spirit carries the Word to areas in our hearts where we harbor resentments just as medicine travels in the physical body to the designated area of need. In Chapter Four, we will look further into resentments and how they serve as strongholds, keeping us in bondage to toxic relationships.

We were designed by God to hunger and thirst after righteousness, yet many of us have spent years hungering and thirsting after whatever made us feel good, whatever provided temporary satisfaction. How long will we eat dirt? trying to instantly gratify our spiritual thirst with physical means. Is your vision obscured? Have you been misled by mirages?

A WORD FROM THE LORD: (*Isaiah 49:9-10) You who are bound and in spiritual darkness, Come-forth – Show yourselves. I promise you shall not hunger nor thirst anymore; Neither will mirage mislead you. For I will have mercy on you and will lead you by the springs of water.*

NOTES AND PRAYERS

CHAPTER III:

TEMPTATION IS SURE TO COME

They gave him vinegar to drink mingled with gall and when he had tasted thereof, he would not drink [Matt 27:34]

CRUCIFIXION IS PAINFUL

Now I wish I could give you a deep revelation on how to let go of toxic relationships without discomfort. The truth is, you either suffer the perpetual pain of being in toxic relationships or you experience the productive pain of letting go. Healing pain is productive because it leads to wholeness. We tend to hold on to what is painfully familiar due to fear of the unknown. When you let go of your toxic ways and ultimately let go of toxic people, there is bound to be discomfort, you may actually miss the pain. Instinctively we want to reach for something to take the edge off and ease the pain. When we are in toxic relationships, we alter our mind and our mood, getting intoxicated to avoid discomforts of life. God is a rewarder of those who diligently seek Him however, His rewards are often gradual and lack the instant gratification of our human, fleshly desires. If we are to experience the rewards God has for us, the healing and deliverance and the plans He has for us, we must defer our need for instant gratification. This is why we must do as Jesus did: go through the crucifixion experience.

As we read the 27th Chapter of the Gospel according to Matthew, starting with vs. 32, it talks about the cross experience of Jesus Christ as he approaches a place called Golgotha, that is to say, the place of the skull. This is just before he gave up the ghost, He died, surrendering His natural life. The writer tells us that Jesus was offered a potion referred to as vinegar solution mixed with gall. (A STUPEFIED POTION, purposed to daze, confuse, befuddle, and bewilder). Matthew reports that when Jesus tasted this stupefied potion, he would not drink. This potion was designed to minimize his pain in that it was composed of wine and an opiate based substance just like many of today's pain relievers are, such as Morphine, Vicodin, prescription Tylenol and Heroin. When a person was being executed by way of crucifixion, it was customary to offer this potion to intoxicate and help alleviate the suffering. Satan offered Jesus an opportunity to numb his pain. Jesus chose to refuse the stupefied potion so that he could endure his cross experience and pay the full penalty for sin, sober and in his right mind. He bore his cross for the joy set before Him, to fulfill his purpose which was the redemption of mankind.

ARE YOU GETTING HIGH ON RELATIONSHIPS? [REFUSE THE STUPEFIED POTION]

The enemy's job is to tempt you. After a period of freedom or even while you are still crucifying your flesh, he will tempt you. The enemy attempted to get Jesus to come down off of the cross and prove Himself to be the Son of God. It is the same with us, we will be taunted and tempted by the enemy. Take up your cross and follow him, deny self-gratification otherwise we are not worthy of him (*Matt. 10:38*). Death by the cross is excruciatingly painful, it is the equivalent of saying 'no' to satanic or unhealthy passions with desires and habits. Just before Jesus gave up the ghost (died) - He said "I thirst."

Satan who was seeking to take advantage of Jesus' vulnerable and seemingly desperate state, offered Jesus a strong drink once again. That strong drink did not have the ability to address the thirst, although it was wet, it was bitter rather than cool and refreshing. Every time we resist the enemy, deny our desire for instant gratification, totally mortify our flesh and just before we get the victory, we thirst!

Satan offers us a temporal solution, promising to numb the pain or take the edge off, if we will just compromise God's word and God's will for us. Jesus proclaimed to be king and according to *Prov. 31:6*, '*strong drink is not for kings; therefore, Satan offered him strong drink to disprove him as king.'*

The enemy wants to prove you to be anything but who God says you are; his goal is to steal, kill and destroy your opportunity to fulfill the purpose for which you were born. Jesus was born to pay the price for our sins and redeem us from the hand of the enemy. He was born to die unblemished and without sin. What if he had taken the stupefied potion? He would not have accomplished his purpose. What is your stupefied potion? Remember, to be stupefied is to be dazed, confused, befuddled, and bewildered. What does the enemy offer you every time you try to overcome your easily besetting sin? What is it that gratifies your flesh and intoxicates you? What stupefies you? Ask the father to give you a glimpse of the joy in overcoming the bondage of that underlying issue which keeps you bound to relationships.

PRIDE COMES BEFORE A FALL: "CAUGHT UP AGAIN! WHAT HAPPENED?"

Satan likes to play the cat and mouse game. He allows us to feel free; he will encourage us to feel powerful, especially if you are the one who said 'goodbye' first. A cat plays with his prey, letting it run freely in a small radius but soon as it gets out too far, he slaps it back into range. In your past efforts to get free, have you experienced a few days or even weeks of freedom and then suddenly, "bam, Caught up again?" You find yourself saying, "I don't know what happened." Well, here is what happened. The book of James 1:14 (*Amp*) says," …'*every person is tempted when drawn away and enticed and baited by his own evil desires (lusts, passions)*'. This lust is referring to a desire so overwhelming that it leads to ungodly decisions and actions, if necessary, to obtain the object of the lust. When we harbor lusts in our hearts, it serves as bait for Satan's hook, by which he reels us in.

In chapter one, we discussed the first Key to Freedom from toxic relationships which was Honesty. Let's look at the second Key to Freedom which is Humility. To humble oneself means to simply agree with God and His Word, disagree with our fleshly desires, and make sure our actions match our decisions. Satan comes to appeal to the ego and other emotional issues. You may thirst to feel powerful, better than, in control, needed, wanted, liked, accepted, etc. You may long to have the other person see how well you are doing without them. This may even lead to getting in debt by purchasing new items to feel like you are better off without them. You may be resentful and want to seek revenge. Feelings of rejection may lead you to seek another relationship to prove to yourself and others that you are worth having. Whatever your feelings tell you, there is a need to humbly submit your feelings and actions to God.

These feelings and actions are issues that give place to the enemy; therefore, the Lord will begin to reveal them to you and deal with you about letting Him fight your battles. Your willingness to cooperate with the Holy Spirit concerning these strongholds determines whether or not you obtain and maintain deliverance. Refusal to surrender these issues to the Lord says that you disagree with His Word. This is where you rise up in pride, declaring "I want what I want, when I want it! I know what I'm doing – I can handle this! I'm grown!" Deliverance depends on our willingness to humble ourselves under the mighty hand of God so that He may raise us up in due season. '*Pride is the opposite of humility, and it goes before destruction and a haughty spirit before a fall.*' (*Prov. 16:18*) This is a principle which applies to all of us; no one can get around it.

Humility is a powerful spiritual warfare weapon. It is used like camouflage is used in the Army. All areas of the flesh that are not covered by the soldier's fatigues must be covered with a black camouflage solution designed to conceal the heat in the flesh. The enemy has infra-red lights on their firearm targeting the flesh, so even in the night they can spot a human. Our flesh screams to reveal itself, when something happens that attaches itself to a stronghold from within, particularly when you feel taunted and provoked by someone, especially the person you were in the relationship with. You begin to overheat in your soul. Here is where we must maintain an attitude of humility and not be moved into responding out of our emotions. Also, here is where we must submit our emotions to the Holy Spirit and remain hidden under the mantle of humility.

This is the position where we should drink the water of the Word of God and allow that water to wash us and cool us down. This is where we hide under the shadow of the almighty. We know that the weapons of our warfare are not carnal but mighty through God for the pulling down of strongholds. We are fighting a spiritual battle which breeds spiritual conflict in our daily life struggles; and many of those struggles are internal. Our greatest struggle is keeping our garments on and standing fast in the midst of the battle. We may put on the right clothing but when the battle rages and the heat is on, instead of maintaining our position, our posture of humility, we forget everything and run out from under the mantle of humility. When you are striving for deliverance, you are in the midst of the heat of the battle. Be careful to be led by the Spirit of God so that you do not gratify the lust of the flesh. Keep in mind that the heat from the battle causes dehydration and mirages, images of living water (solutions) that are actually poisonous to the soul. Remember, dehydrated people in the desert see mirages of pools of water and rescuers because that is what they need. Do not be fooled, the heat from the battle also causes overheating, exhaustion, and battle fatigue. As a result, you may feel like giving up; but keep your clothes on and do not resort to old ways and habits. Do not be weary in doing well for you will reap in due season if you faint not.

Humble yourself to do it God's way by presenting your body a living sacrifice, for this is your reasonable worship. When God says, "Don't call", DON'T! When He says, "Be Still", BE STILL! When He says, "Be Quiet", BE QUIET! Right there, submit to God with an attitude of humility; yes, it hurts in the moment but in due season you shall reap if you faint not. Stand firm in the liberty, the freedom wherewith God has set you free and do not be entangled in the same bondage. Remember, the Holy Spirit is a temperature regulator. If we obey His leadings, He cools us down internally and flushes the impurities out of us just as water does naturally in the form of perspiration, then we begin to bear the fruit of temperance.

We receive Grace to help us in our time of need. Grace, Grace, Grace – God gives Grace to the Humble. When we humble ourselves and run to the Throne of Grace to ask for God's help to keep us from acting out in our old ways, we receive grace. Grace is the power we need to meet the evil tendencies of this age (*Heb. 4:16 - Amp*).

GRACE CHANGES

Grace changed Saul from a Persecutor of the Church into the Apostle Paul (*1 Cor. 15:10*). When Saul met Christ on Damascus Road, he humbled himself by agreeing that Jesus was Lord and by God's Grace and Power, Saul was changed into Paul (*Acts 9:1-31*). We see another account of the Power of Grace with Noah in *Genesis 6:8*, this passage says Noah found grace in the sight of God. Noah agreed to do the will of God by building the Ark and he and his family were saved from the destruction of the flood, Grace saves from destruction. *Genesis 19:19* gives us another account of Grace, Lot found grace with God as he agreed to leave Sodom, although his human emotions and his flesh wanted to stay; he also was saved from destruction.

Grace is God's unmerited favor; it is undeserved, but it must be obtained through humbling ourselves by agreeing with God and disagreeing with our ungodly desires. If we allow those underlying issues of anger, rejection, loneliness, hurt, disappointment, fear, resentment or any other stronghold to rule us, then our position becomes one of self-willed worship instead of worshiping God with our obedience. When our attitude rules, we position ourselves in a posture of pride and arrogance rather than one of humility. An attitude of "I can handle this one God!" will cause us to proceed with carnal methods of handling a situation our own way. This is pride and God resists pride.

We are instructed in *1 Peter 5:5* to be clothed in humility; cover ourselves with the mantle of humility and hide our flesh under the covering of humility and this will counteract pride. God resists the proud and gives grace to the humble. The mantle of humility covers all flesh and prevents the enemy from spotting you. Satan hits flesh and targets pride. When we operate in our fleshly desires, we operate in pride. A prideful attitude causes God to resist us. To be humble is to obey God's Word and His direction in spite of our ideas or beliefs. As we crucify our flesh, surrendering to God's will, we experience deliverance from the strongholds of our old ideas and beliefs. We begin to operate with a renewed mind with God's ideas and beliefs according to His Word. As long as we remain humble, continuing to do battle with the enemy clothed in the mantle of humility towards one another, Satan cannot pick us up on his infrared radar, or should we say, his "flesh finder." *Psalms 91* tells us that '*he who dwells in the secret place of the Most-High, shall abide under the shadow of the Almighty...He is our refuge and our fortress, Our God, in Him shall we Trust.*' When you maintain the posture of humility, trusting Him, you are hidden under the shadow of the Almighty. However, because He resists pride, pride causes God to keep us at a distance, but He extends grace to the humble; allowing us to come close enough to hide in His shadow. Think about it, to get in someone's shadow you have got to get close to them. I want to make sure I make it plain. When we disregard God's Word, allowing flesh to dictate us, we are resisted by God, operating outside of His shadow, and revealed to the enemy. The enemy picks us up on his infrared radar and he sees the heat of your emotions. Operating outside of God's shadow reveals our position to the enemy and he has a legal right to hit our flesh. Hear this people of God, the wicked one is looking for a target to shoot his fiery darts. When we trust in self-will and the ways of the world instead of having faith in God to work it out His way, we have stepped out from behind the shield of faith. Flesh is revealed and 'BAM, HIT AGAIN!'

SELF-DECEPTION TACTICS:

Common to all addictions is the term 'self-deception.' Here are a few tips to assist in breaking free from a cycle of deceiving oneself. Satan's job is to tempt you. After a period of freedom from the toxic relationship, expect him to return. The same person or a new one will show up saying all the right things and doing things that appeal to your flesh and your pride. Watch out for these three traps: Rationalization, Idealization and Unfounded Hope.

Rationalization is the technique of giving yourself good reason that conceals your underlying motive to continue the toxic relationship. For example, "I can't leave them because they stayed with me when I was at my lowest-low." This sounds so unselfish and caring, but the truth is you do not want to let go of the instant gratification you get from the relationship. It could be sex, care-taking, feeling needed, or financial security. I will bet that if you check yourself, you will find a motive, '*And that's ok, just own your stuff*!' Then there is idealization and justification, this is a double hit tactic. Idealization is living in an illusion of who you want this person to be, exaggerating their good points and diminishing the negative ones, in an effort to have the positive outweigh the negative to justify staying in the relationship.

Let us not forget unfounded hope. This is the self-deception tactic of hoping without any supporting evidence upon which to base the hope. You want to stay so you allow smooth speech or lip service to serve as a sign that there is reason to hope for better, knowing full well you have heard it all before. Check your heart; because according to *James 1:14* you can only be led astray by the lust in your own heart. Sincere hope for the relationship must be built upon consistent actions leading towards change, from both parties; change from self-will and self-centeredness into God's will being at the center of the relationship. Sometimes we say, "Go away, it's over!", however, our actions say, "STAY!" Or we say, "No!" but our actions say, "Yes!" It is time to resist the devil, submit to God and the devil will flee. If you feel that you are trying to change things in your life, but things seem to be staying the same, check for ways in which you have agreed with the devil and resisted God. Therein lies the answer to your dilemma. Turn it around, agree with God, resist the devil because he is the enemy within.

TOXIC RELATIONSHIP FLASHBACKS

"Needed or Being Used"

It must be me doing something wrong. I cannot seem to please my man. I have done all I know to do, but he is still mad. It must be me. I must be behaving badly.

Why is my man so mad? Did I let him down? Should I dye my hair, lose weight? Surely that will make him happy. Maybe I will cook his favorite meal.

I do not know, cannot figure it out. I tried all I know and he is still looking pouty. It is my job to make him alright; better hurry up before he starts a fight.

Baby what's wrong? What can I do? Girl, give me some money! that's what I need from you. Oh, so glad I made my man smile. He needs me so much

I will rest 'cause I have been good to my man. I have been the very best that I can be.

My question to you is: IS THAT LIVING?

"Loving Being Hated"

Oh, my sweet fine man, I will do anything for you, just do
not leave me.
Oh, I know you really care about me, 'cause you are
worried when I am gone.
If you did not care, you would not spank me when I am
wrong.
Oh, my sweet fine man, your dinner is done and the water
is ready for your bath.
Let me scrub your big fine back. Oh, don't fret about the
bruise on my face; I know you would not hit me if I
would have stayed in my place, just do not leave
me.
Oh, sweet fine man, can I rub your tired feet?
Oh, I am fine, do not worry about me, I know what you say
ain't what you really mean.

You just slipped when you talked badly to me; I know you
really wanted to say how much you love me instead.

Oh, my sweet fine man please stay; do not leave me.

Again, my question to you is: ***"WHAT'S LOVE GOT TO DO WITH THAT?"***

These are flashbacks from my own toxic mindset and are from a woman's perspective. However, try to see the spirit of the message. *II Timothy Chapter 3* tells us that *"in the last days there will be a silly spirit that will lead astray those burdened with various lusts."* It is this lust, an overwhelmingly strong desire, perhaps for affection, attention, companionship, etc., in the hearts of both men and women that causes us to be silly enough to follow and even persuade abusive people to stay with us.

That silly spirit allows us to welcome unhealthy situations. Referring again briefly to *Ezekiel 16:33 (TLB)*, "*Prostitutes charge for their services – but not you! You give gifts to your lovers, bribing them to come to you."*

According to *James 1:22*, we are instructed to *"be doers of the Word of God, not hearers only, for if we hear and refuse to do, we deceive only ourselves."* The Word of God is a mirror. In this same passage of scripture, it is referred to as a glass into which we behold ourselves. The Word will reveal to you the nature of your wrong-doings as well as the strongholds that have kept you bound. Obedience to God's Word is our road map to abundant life. As we move into Chapter Four, more of your participation is required, therefore, "It is Time to Work!"

NOTES AND PRAYERS

CHAPTER IV:

THE FINAL ESCAPE

For He (Father God) has rescued us out of the darkness and gloom of Satan's kingdom and brought us into the Kingdom of His dear Son, who bought our freedom with His blood and forgave us all our sins (Col. 1:13-14 TLB)

THE CYCLE OF MISERY

The past has power over us if we choose to stay stuck there. We can, however, choose to use it for our good or we can continue to allow it to disrupt our daily lives and dictate our future. Our perceptions and feelings directly affect our choices. We have been transformed out of the darkness of the past and brought into the Kingdom of Christ who paid for our freedom with His blood, forgiving us of all our sins. If we continue to dwell on the injustices of our past, we will stay in what is referred to by the Narcotics Anonymous IP, pamphlet #12 as a 'triangle of self-obsession'. **(Narcotics Anonymous IP, pamphlet #12)**

DISARMING THE POWER OF THE PAST

THE CYCLE OF MISERY

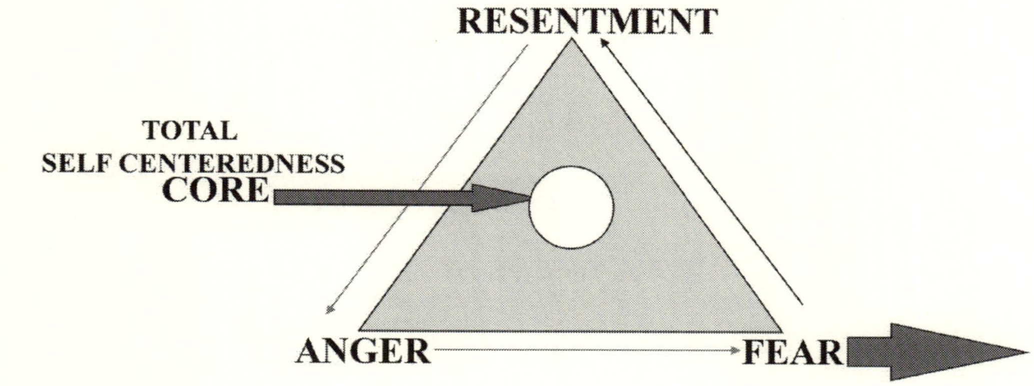

The angles of the triangle, as you can see in the diagram, are as follows: the top angle is 'resentment', the right angle is 'fear' and the left angle is 'anger.' I've labeled the core of this cycle 'total self-centeredness,' which by the way is identified in the 12-Step program as the core of the disease of addiction; toxic relationships equal another addiction. This core is the stronghold causing us to remain in the vicious cycle of dwelling in the injustices of our past.

When we are caught in this cycle, three things tend to happen: (i) our resentments are our reactions to our past, (ii) anger is our response to our present situations, and (iii) fear is our reaction to our future. Again, the concept of this triangle is used in the 12-step program and it is not just exclusive to substance abusers. We stay stuck in self-pity, feeling sorry for ourselves because of the things that have happened to us as well as the mistakes we have made. Self-Centeredness is the core of this cycle. Think about a skin-boil. When the doctor lances it, he digs or cuts until he gets the core out, otherwise, it will continue to come back. Our future is hindered by resentful feelings concerning the past. We look at our current position in life and feel angry, declaring that if we had just done things differently, or if that had not happened to us, our lives would be much better.

The future looks bleak as we explore possibilities for change because we are still basing what can happen on what already has or should have happened and did not. Perhaps we find ourselves saying. Things like "If I would've; Wish I could've". Once caught in this vicious cycle, we never move into God's best for our lives because we go from being resentful of the past to being angry about the present and fearful of the future; therefore, we end up back to resentment again rather than moving out of the cycle of misery with faith. We can disarm the power of the past, if we do what the Word of God says and forgive ourselves and others. Forgiveness is a conscious decision and a process. If we refuse to allow God to help us remove the core, then we will continue to malfunction. The Word of God says that God promises to use what the devil meant for evil and turn it around for our good. We must ask God to give us eyes to see what He sees; and an ear to hear what He hears concerning our past, then it will work to our advantage and for our future. Let's look at disarming the power of the past.

DISARMING THE POWER OF THE PAST

To forgive, is to stop blaming or feeling resentment towards someone (self-included); and/or to grant pardon to someone or something that was done wrongfully. Resentment is anger and ill-will caused by a feeling of injury or mistreatment or to hold a grudge. There are situations that you thought you had overcome. Maybe it happened so long ago, that you knew you had forgotten them; however, just like an old sore with a scab on it, you think it is healed until you bump it and it bleeds again. That is when you realize it was deeper than you thought. Our emotional wounds also bleed when we bump them, for example: when that person shows up unexpectedly, or perhaps when that time of the year rolls around; or maybe someone is wearing the same cologne/perfume that that person once wore. When your stomach flips and your mood is suddenly altered, you need to recognize that Satan is attempting to take you captive at his will.

According to *II Timothy 2:25-26*, people who oppose themselves may receive repentance from God (if God so chooses) if they will acknowledge the Truth, they may recover themselves out of the snare of the devil, after being overtaken by him at his will. To disarm the power of the past, we must honestly admit what we feel. This means we must be honest in our confession, calling it exactly what it is. Saying, "Help me with these feelings," is too vague. We must identify the feeling, if at all possible. "Help me, I feel _____________ [Fill in the blank]. What did you feel? Hate, hurt, unforgiveness, rejection, mistreatment, disappointment, disrespected; name it and fill in the blank. This is what we must do. Sometimes, it is difficult to admit to God, your accountability partner, and even sometimes to yourself, how hurt you are really feeling. This requires humility, which we discussed in Chapter III. Again, humility is the opposite of pride. Becoming willing to abandon our own plans and approach the situation in a new way is what is needed. Instead of saying, "she/he didn't hurt me, I'm fine," we can say "I've been hurt and I feel _______________ (fill in the blank). I can't get past this by myself. I need help." These are honest admissions that we must make, if you cannot get honest, then you cannot get free.

There are physical, emotional, and spiritual consequences for holding a grudge. Bitterness can cause a chemical imbalance, inflicting great physical damage to the body. This results in ulcers, high blood pressure, and other diseases. Bitterness causes the pituitary, adrenal, thyroid, and other glands to produce too many hormones; an excess of these hormones will collect in the organs and form pockets, causing diseases. In addition, harboring unforgiveness can create an emotional focus towards the one we resent, causing us to become just like the person who hurt us. Hurting people, hurt people. How is that encouragement to forgive? Do we want to become just like the ones who hurt us? No!

Depression is another emotional response that we may have in response to holding on to resentments. It requires emotional energy to maintain a grudge, eventually leading to emotional exhaustion. Months, even years, after a situation takes place, we may find ourselves re-living it and rehearsing what we should have said and how we should have said it. This is called letting someone live rent free in your head.

In Apostle Paul's second letter to the Corinthians he said, "*it is true that I am an ordinary, weak human being, but I do not use human plans and methods to win my battles. I use God's mighty weapons, not those made by men, to knock down the devil's strongholds. These weapons can break down every proud argument against God and every wall that can be built to keep men from finding him. With these weapons I can capture rebels and bring them back to God and change them into men whose hearts' desire is obedience to Christ.*" (*2 Cor. 10:3-5 TLB*). I told you that resentments affect us in three ways. We have discussed the physical and emotional effects, now let's look at the spiritual. The scripture above says that there are walls built to keep men from finding God. We must use spiritual weapons to break down these walls and every proud argument against God. When we hold resentments, we actually display pride because we disregard God's Word which says, "*you have heard that it was said, 'You shall love your neighbor and hate your enemy', but I say to you, love your enemies, bless those who curse you, do good to those who hate you, and pray for those who spitefully use you and persecute you*" (*Matt. 5:43-44 NKJV*).

This rebellion causes a wall of resentment to be formed and the enemy uses it to keep us from truly finding God. Resentments also keep us from receiving forgiveness from God, as his Word says in *Mark 11:25-26* "*and when you stand praying, forgive if you have strife against any, that your Father also which is in heaven may forgive you your trespasses. But if you do not forgive, neither will your Father which is in heaven forgive your trespasses."*

As you have been reading this chapter, you have thought about people and situations from your past. This is the Holy Spirit bringing to your remembrance what you need to deal with. The upcoming diagrams are two resentment walls; the first one is an example and the second one is your assignment. Each rectangular shape is a brick in the wall. Use this as your personal resentment wall, putting one name per brick, of people who have harmed, disappointed or offended you in any way.

Remember to include yourself and God (if necessary). For example: 'I resented God for some of the things He allowed me to go through, so I had to put Him on my wall' and 'I was angry at myself for some of the choices I made, so I had to put myself on the wall.' In a natural brick wall, there must be mortar to hold the bricks together to form the wall, and so it is with this spiritual brick wall. These isolated incidents have come together to form a resentment wall, held together by the offenses.

Some examples of offenses are seen below: abandonment, betrayal, abuse, embarrassment, and rejection, just to name a few. Take this time to complete your wall.

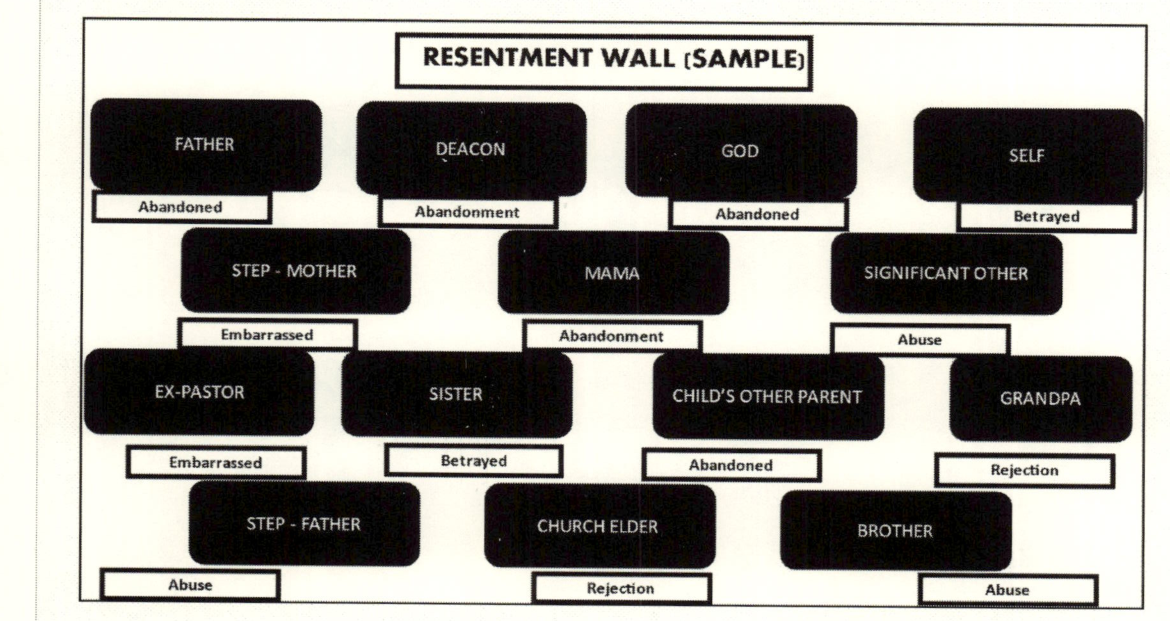
RESENTMENT WALL (SAMPLE)
FATHER
Abandoned
DEACON
Abandonment
GOD
Abandoned
SELF
Betrayed
STEP - MOTHER
Embarrassed
MAMA
Abandonment
SIGNIFICANT OTHER
Abuse
EX-PASTOR
Embarrassed
SISTER
Betrayed
CHILD'S OTHER PARENT
Abandoned
GRANDPA
Rejection
STEP - FATHER
Abuse
CHURCH ELDER
Rejection
BROTHER
Abuse

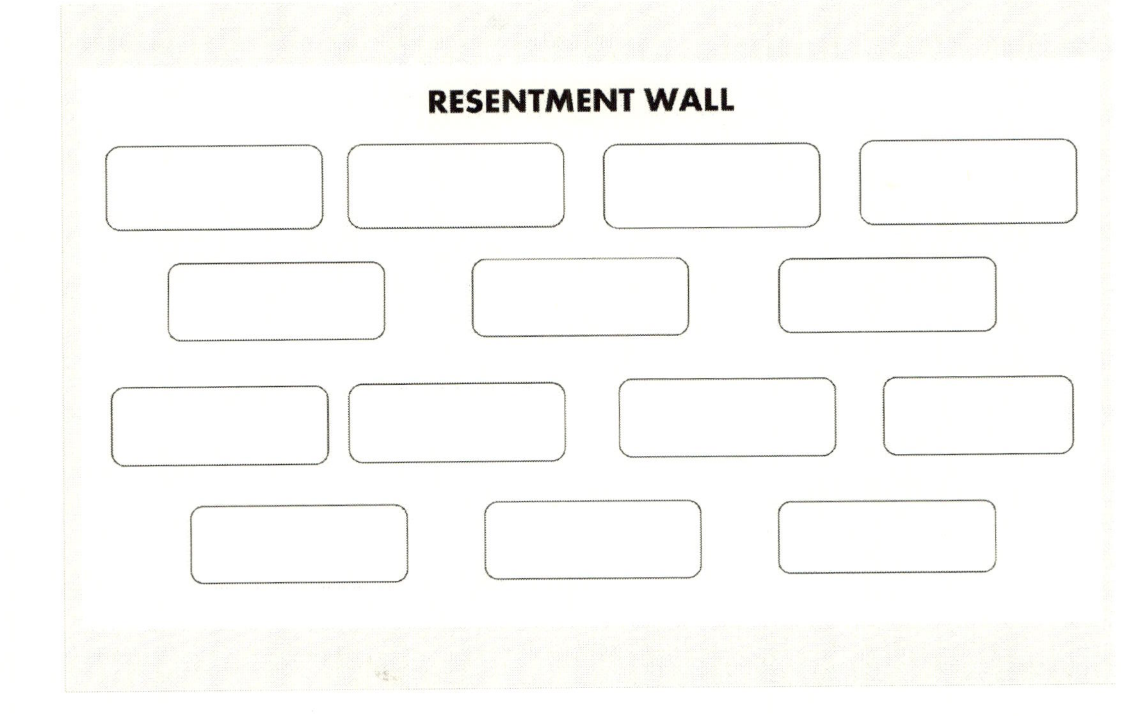
RESENTMENT WALL

Could any of these resentments from the past be affecting your choices and your interaction in relationships today? Does your past dictate your future? If you answered "yes", you're on the right track, keep reading.

Have you had (or do you have) any relationships you try to control to keep from being hurt? Grab your journal and begin to write your feelings. Now may be a good time to call your accountability partner. Remember, your accountability partner should not be the opposite sex or your sexual preference.

After you have completed your wall, begin to destroy the wall that hinders your spiritual growth by being a doer of the Word and not a hearer only. This is where you obey the Word of God in *Matthew 5:43-44*, Pray for those who you named in the bricks on your resentment wall. This will not be easy but it is necessary to break free. Although you may not understand how this will destroy the wall, open your mind to this new way in which the Word of God is instructing you. God's ways are not yours, neither are his thoughts your thoughts. It is important that you utilize what you have learned so far. You have practiced two of the six spiritual principles needed to destroy this wall; Honesty and Humility. The other four are Open-Mindedness, Trust, Willingness and Forgiveness. You have honestly named those who hurt you and humbly identified what they did to cause pain. So now that you have been honest and humble, you must be open-minded enough to trust God and forgive.

There are two types of forgiveness: willful forgiveness and emotional forgiveness. You may not 'feel' the desire to forgive in your emotions, however, you can begin the process by an act of your will. Let's do a demonstration. I am going to tell you to do something; here it goes – "STAND UP" – Go ahead, STAND UP!!! More than likely, you were relaxing and had no intention or desire to stand up at this time. If you did it, then it was an act of your will. This is how you willfully forgive; you do it in spite of how you feel. Ask God to help you, admit that you cannot do it in your own strength (this is humbling).

Your prayer should be as simple as "God, help (their name goes here) to be a better person." Eventually you may be able to say, "God forgive them for what they did to me." Here you have practiced another spiritual principle which is Willingness. As you continue to pray for them (and you must be diligent to do so), you will begin to release the resentments felt towards them. You will find that the mention of their name or the smell of the cologne they wore no longer has the ability to take you captive. The cycle of misery comes to an end because you no longer have resentments. You are no longer angry regarding your current condition and the fear of the future is dissipating. You can now move forward.

TOOLS FOR BREAKING THE RELATIONSHIP ADDICTION

If you are in a relationship right now, the previous exercise will have brought you some clarity. You can begin to see the true condition of your current relationship. Your perception will no longer be clouded by your past resentments and your fears of the future will have lessened. You may have once felt that living without a significant other was impossible; you will now be able to see yourself letting go of unhealthy situations. We often say, "Just let go and let God." That is certainly an excellent suggestion, however, we may not know how, therefore, here are a few tips:

1. Pray for God to give you eyes to see what He sees and ears to hear what He hears concerning His will for your life.

2. Keep a Relationship Journal. Write down the details of the relationship; the good times and the rough times.

---

3. Document your feelings when things are good and when they are not. This will help you by having selective memory meaning remembering only what feels good and discounting the situations that have been abusive and/or unacceptable.

4. Reflect on past relationships. Document similarities in people and situations. Ask God to search and reveal to you, your true heart's intent. God's Word says that we are drawn away by the lust in our own heart and enticed. What is continually drawing you into the same types of situations?

5. Identify situations you put up with or put yourself in, to maintain the relationship; situations that you feel are morally wrong or unhealthy. When your values and your behaviors do not line up, it lowers your self-esteem.

6. Keep a chart, rating the following as Good, Fair or Poor

---

a. My partner's ability to enhance my spiritual well being

b. Two-way communication

c. My trust towards my significant other

d. My significant other's trust towards me

e. Their commitment towards God (evidenced by a conscious effort towards a lifestyle of obedience to God's Word)

f. My commitment towards God (same evidence)

g. Respect towards one another

h. Shared interest

i. Emotional Support

You may also think of some other points you want to keep a record of in your journal as situations in the relationship arise. These points may serve as areas of focus for improving the relationship, if both parties are on board to work on improving. Review your journal entries weekly. You should be able to make a decision concerning the action needed. Where you were once stuck, you will now be free to change. Your vision is no longer obstructed. The living water of the Word of God has corrected your dehydrated state of thirst. Change is uncomfortable, even painful at times. Humans are creatures of habit and when we break habits, we often experience emotional upheavals. Chapter V will assist in maintaining your position of freedom.

NOTES AND PRAYERS: Grab your pen and begin to address these tips, as the Lord reveals your heart to you:

____

____

____

____

____

____

____

____

____

____

____

____

____

____

____

____

____

CHAPTER V:

MAINTAINING A POSITION OF FREEDOM

"Be not entangled again in the same yoke of bondage wherewith Christ has set you free." (Gal. 5:1)

Once you are free to grow and enter into the light of life that God has in store for you, you will need to live a life conducive to remaining your freedom. *St. John 10:10* tells us that *"Satan comes to kill, steal, and destroy, but God has come to give you life and that more abundantly."* This chapter will assist you in maintaining your position of freedom.

SPIRITUAL PRINCIPLES FOR SETTING BOUNDARIES

The same principles you practiced to obtain freedom must be used to maintain that freedom. You will need to continue your relationship with your accountability partner, and you may want to add others who are free from toxic relationships, to your support network. You must remain honest in your practices with others. Here is a suggestion; if you cannot practice honesty in all of your affairs, change your affairs. In other words, if you cannot tell it, do not do it. Your commitment to honesty will help you make healthier choices. Remaining humble in every situation will keep you out of false pride and arrogance. Remember, pride goes before destruction and a haughty spirit before a fall. Remaining humble simply means agreeing with God's way and disagreeing with your flesh. Do not obey your flesh, it is in cahoots with the devil.

Open-mindedness is vital to your maintenance because you are accustomed to doing things a certain way. For instance, you may have always felt comfortable accepting money from someone who you were not interested in, but knew they were interested in you. Your belief may have been, "well if they have money to give away, I'll take it." However, now that you're committed to remaining free from entanglement, you will be required to change your way of dealing. This will require open-mindedness to trust in God. As you change, remember there is a way that seems right to you but eventually that way ends in destruction. You have addressed your resentment. You will need to work at ongoing forgiveness to avoid developing new resentments. Wouldn't it be nice if nothing ever happens to hurt you again and then you would not need to forgive? Well, we know that is unrealistic. We must practice the spiritual principle of forgiveness weekly, daily, maybe even minute by minute. If we commit to not letting the sun go down on our anger, we will address situations as they occur. If it cannot be addressed directly with the person of interest, call someone in your support circle, pray about it and write about it – but do not hold it in.

"To whom you forgive anything, I forgive also...lest Satan should get an advantage of us; for we are not ignorant of his devices." (*2 Cor. 2:10-12*). Practicing spiritual principles will keep you within the boundaries

God has set for you and will guide you into healthy relationships.

DON'T BE IGNORANT OF THE DEVIL'S DEVICES

Danger approaches oftentimes in subtle and crafty ways. We have an adversary who is roaming about seeking whom he may devour. If you know how to recognize him, then you will be less likely to be devoured. In fact, once you truly know the devices of the devil, you cannot be tricked (even if you wanted to be)! The devil's goal is to get us to disagree with God and agree with him, getting us into disobedience. It is our disobedience that may allow him to trap us and take us captive at his will. The Word of God says that when the devil departed from Jesus in the wilderness that it was only for a season, a measure of time. We too can expect him to return to us after a season of freedom. Now that you are changing and experiencing a measure of freedom, do not be surprised when old desires and thoughts return. Here are some things to watch-out for:

COMMONLY USED DEVICES OF THE DEVIL

Conversation: You may hear enticing conversation either in your own thoughts or from another person. The conversation will discredit God's Truth, telling you that you can beat the odds, i.e., 'You don't have to stop – just be more careful this time'. You may hear conversations that promise advantages or downplay the danger involved, i.e., 'If you just keep on for a while longer, they will see the blessing in being with you and leave their spouse' or 'One more time won't hurt, no one will find out.' Communication is a device the serpent used on Eve in the garden, "*Did God really say, "You must not eat from any tree in the garden"? "You will not certainly die,*" the serpent said to the woman. "*For God knows that when you eat from it your eyes will be opened, and you will be like God, knowing good and evil.*" (Gen. 3:1,4,5) To "know" in this scripture is to "be intimate with" just as Adam "knew"

Eve and she conceived! You don't want to be intimate with evil and conceive - now do you?

Distraction: You may receive a phone call or a visit. Your ears and eyes are gateways to your soul. Your soul is the area of your mind, will and emotions. The area of your soul is where the enemy wants to communicate with you. When God's people were rebuilding the temple in Ezra 4th chapter, the bible says, "*When the enemies of Judah and Benjamin heard that the exiles were building a temple for the Lord, they came to Zerubbabel and to the heads of the families and said, Let us help you build because like you, we seek your God...*" Child of God, you are building a temple for the Lord, please know that your body is the temple of the Holy Spirit. When the person you need to separate from (or someone who is useful to the devil), takes interest in your God all of a sudden, even wanting to study with you – BEWARE!

Frustration: As they continued to build the temple for the Lord, *Ezra 4:4* says, "*The people around them set out to discourage the people of Judah and make them afraid to go on building. They hired counselors to work against them and frustrate their plans;" Can* you believe that the enemy hires counselors to frustrate your plans as you seek to grow and rebuild the temple of God - as you seek to rebuild your life? Who does the enemy hire? Anyone available. When we are not submitted to God, we are unable to resist the devil (*James 4:7*); this makes us available for the enemy's use. When you make a decision to change your lifestyle for God's glory and you begin to rebuild the temple, your adversary, the devil, will use who and whatever he can to hinder the work.

Discouragement: In *Ezra 4:13*, the enemy wrote a letter to the king indicating that if the people of God were allowed to continue restoring the walls and repairing the foundation, no more revenues, taxes or duty would be paid and the royal revenues would suffer. To prevent this, the enemy suggested to the king that the archives (those old dead files) be searched to find information useful in justifying opposition to the rebuilding of the temple. In other words, the enemy will dig up your past and attempt to use it to discourage you. He hopes you will feel unworthy and hopeless, return to your old behavior and give up on building a new life.

Flattery: Sweet talk, smooth speech that appeals to one's ego, lusts, and false pride, this is flattery. The bible speaks of a vile, despicable man who is not in line for royal succession but slips in when least expected and takes over the kingdom with flattery and intrigue. He gave the people riches to fool them into trusting him (*Dan 11*). This same description of cunningness and craftiness is used to describe Satan (*Gen. 3*). Your adversary will use flattery to manipulate you and sway you from the Truth. We see in *Daniel chapter 11* that the people violated the covenant and became corrupt with flattery. In order to be manipulated through flattery, one must violate the covenant agreement with God; one must be drawn away by the lust in their own hearts and enticed. Whatever you have agreed to in covenant with God, is what the enemy is after.

We see, conversation, distraction, frustration, discouragement, and flattery are various devices used by Satan to hinder your growth. Here are some tips for safeguarding against those devices:

TIPS FOR SAFEGUARDING AGAINST THE DEVIL'S DEVICES

1. "*Neither give place to the devil*" (*Eph. 4:27*). Do not set yourself up by putting confidence in your flesh, because no good thing dwells in it. Make up your mind not to put yourself in the convenient position to do what you said you were not going to do again.

2. Do not test yourself - you do not have to prove you are delivered. In the wilderness, the devil told Jesus to prove He was the Son of God and Jesus said, "*Thou shall not tempt the Lord thy God*" (*Luke 4:12*)

3. Does "what if," "if only," and "just one more time" sound familiar? These are thoughts used by the enemy to get you to feel that you may have made the wrong decision. Do not look back. Lot's wife disobeyed the angel's directions and when she looked back, she was destroyed (read about her in *Gen. 19:19*). Follow God's instructions.

When you read the Word and commune with Him daily, He will direct your steps.

4. Tell yourself "NO!" to instant gratification. Read about Esau and how he gave up his birthright to be instantly gratified (*Heb. 12:16-17*). He cried and begged and could not get back what he had lost. Consider the price of sin; for the wages of sin is death, in other words something is surely going to die such as relationships and/or spiritual growth.

5. Be just as determined to do right as you were to do wrong. Crucifying your flesh is necessary. Do not obey your 'thirst'. Submit to God, resist the devil and the devil will have to flee (*James 4:7*). All ungodly feelings will pass, just lean on God. I remember when He told me to lean on Him because He's got my back!

6. Separate yourself from people whose lifestyles are contrary to your new life. The Lord has said, "*Leave them;*

separate yourselves from them; don't touch their filthy things, and I will welcome you." (*II Cor. 6:17*).

Remember, when Jesus was on the cross, just before He gave up the ghost – just before He took His last human breath, he said, "I Thirst" and the enemy offered Him vinegar and gall (opiate and wine) to numb His pain. Satan wanted to keep Him from fulfilling His purpose. Don't forget that Satan's goal is to keep you from becoming all that God has predestined you to be. Just before you get the victory, he will offer you something to take the edge off and numb the pain. DON'T TAKE IT! It will stupefy you! If you stay on the cross and crucify your flesh, you will be resurrected in greater power and authority to live a victorious life.

DON'T BE MISLED BY MIRAGES - EXPECT TO SEE HIS KINGDOM COME ON EARTH AS IT IS IN HEAVEN – IN YOUR LIFE!

TAKE A STANCE: FOR GOD I LIVE AND FOR GOD I DIE!! WALK OUT YOUR COMMITMENT AND WATCH THE BLESSINGS OF GOD OVERTAKE YOU.

Made in the USA
Middletown, DE
13 March 2022